W0006481

Ruby and the Rubbish Bin

Margot Sunderland

Illustrated by

Nicky Armstrong

Speechmark ⑤

Speechmark Publishing Ltd
Telford Road, Bicester, Oxon OX26 4LQ, UK
www.speechmark.net

Helping Children with Feelings Series
Storybook & Guidebook Sets

First published in 2003 by
Speechmark Publishing Ltd
Telford Road, Bicester, Oxon OX26 4LQ, United Kingdom
Telephone: +44 (0) 1869 244644 Fax: +44 (0) 1869 320040
www.speechmark.net

Text copyright © M Sunderland 2003
Illustrations copyright © N Armstrong 2003

Reprinted 2005

All rights reserved. The whole of this work, including all text and illustrations, is protected by copyright. No part of this work may be loaded, stored, manipulated, reproduced or transmitted in any form or by any means, electronic or mechanical, including photocopying and recording or by any information, storage and retrieval system without prior written permission from the publisher, on behalf of the copyright owners.

002-5146/Printed in Malaysia/2040

British Library Cataloguing in Publication Data
Sunderland, Margot
Ruby and the rubbish bin : a story for children
with low self-esteem. – (Helping children with feelings)
1. Self-esteem – Juvenile fiction.   2. Friendship – Juvenile fiction.
3. Children's stories
I. Title   II. Armstrong, Nicky
823.9'14 (J)

ISBN 0 86388 462 8

Once, there was a little girl called Ruby.

The trouble was . . .
Ruby felt more like a piece of rubbish than a little girl.

Sometimes she felt like something you find in a bin.

Sometimes she felt like something on the pavement that people stand on.

Children in the playground shouted, "Ruby rubbish!"

Big bully boys yelled from the bus, "Stupid-girly-whirly hair." They even dropped their ice-cream wrappers on Ruby's head.

And one of Ruby's teachers, Mrs Fruity-Nose, often picked on Ruby. She told Ruby that she wasn't sitting up straight, wasn't being neat enough, and that she had to try a lot harder.

When Ruby drew a house, she said to herself, "It's a rubbish house," and she scribbled it out. When Ruby drew a tree, she said to herself, "It's a rubbish tree," and she threw it away.

And when Ruby looked at herself in the mirror, she saw a yukky, smelly girl. "You're so ugly," thought Ruby.

After school, Ruby liked hanging around the rubbish bins. She didn't know why she liked it. She just did. Sometimes she even felt like getting into one of the bins and never coming out.

Each Friday, the dustbin men came to empty the rubbish from the bins.

"Hello, sweetie!" said one of them. "I'm not a sweetie," said Ruby, "I'm rubbish."

Each Saturday, Ruby went to the sweet shop to buy some sherbet lemons. "There you are, lovey," said the sweet-shop lady. "I'm not a lovey," said Ruby, "I'm rubbish."

And the last time she was there a little girl said, "I like your hair." "It's stupid-girly-whirly hair," said Ruby. "It's funny," she thought, "how people can get you so wrong."

One day, Ruby's Auntie Flo in Australia sent Ruby some super red and black trainers. Ruby thought they were great.

In fact, for the whole afternoon, Ruby didn't feel rubbish at all. She really felt quite OK. People at school liked her trainers too.

Now the problem with things like trainers is that they don't make you feel good about yourself for very long. And sure enough, when Ruby did her homework that evening and couldn't spell 'sausage' or 'spaghetti', it all came back. "I'm a rubbish speller," said Ruby, "I'm just rubbishy Ruby and that's all there is to it."

And at that moment, Ruby felt so rubbishy that she wanted to sleep and sleep and never wake up again.

Then one day at school, there was a new lunchtime lady called Dot. Dot had just moved into a house in the same street as Ruby.

When Ruby stood in the lunch queue, Dot smiled at Ruby. It was such a lovely smile, that something warm happened in Ruby's tummy.

In fact, Ruby was so surprised by the smile that she dropped her lunch.

"Oh dear, let me help you,"
said Dot the lunchtime lady.

Ruby was so surprised that Dot hadn't called her
'stupid' for dropping her lunch, that she dropped her
pudding too.

"Never mind, sweetheart," said Dot, putting her arm around Ruby. "It's funny how things can go wrong in twos, isn't it?"

Ruby tried to tell Dot that she wasn't a sweetheart, she was rubbish, but it didn't quite come out, because by then she had a big lump in her throat and wanted to cry.

On her way home, Ruby passed by Dot's house. Dot was sitting in her garden in a deck-chair. "Hey Ruby, I've got something for you," said Dot. To Ruby's surprise, Dot had drawn a picture of Ruby with lots of rubbish on her head. "Ruby, some of the nice teachers at school told me about how you think you are rubbish. Well now, I think you've got into a bit of a muddle."

"You see, when some people feel small, they try to make themselves feel big by making other people feel small instead. This is how bullies get made."

"But when it's you they pick on, it makes you feel you're rubbish."

Dot went on crossly, "And if people can't see how lovely you are, that's their loss, not yours."

Ruby didn't really understand this last bit, but it made the warm thing happen in her tummy again.

That night, Ruby had a dream . . .

In her dream, people were piling all sorts of rubbish over her head: stale chips, chewed up bits of pizza and smelly anchovies. Ruby was drowning in the rubbish, and then it got even more horrible because someone mistook Ruby for rubbish and put her in the bin too. It was awful.

But then something amazing happened. In her dream, Ruby suddenly felt very angry, and her anger made her feel so strong . . .

… that she poured the rubbish right back over everyone.

Next day in class, Mrs Fruity-Nose scolded Ruby for too many crossings out. Ted the Tough jeered at her for getting cheese sauce on her sweater, and someone called her stupid for wearing odd socks.

Suddenly, Ruby had had enough.
She remembered her dream.

She stood up. "Excuse me everybody, but let's get one thing straight from now on. I'm not rubbish. In fact, I'm getting really fed up with people who feel bad about themselves trying to make me feel bad instead."

"And if you can't see that I'm lovely, then it's your loss, not mine." Everyone clapped, except for the bullies, who fell over in shock, and Mrs Fruity-Nose, who looked very surprised indeed.

Ruby often visited Dot the lunchtime lady in her garden. They became great friends. Together they would do some gardening and laugh and talk.

It was so much fun, that sometimes it felt to Ruby as if they were flying together.

And when Dot smiled that special smile, or gave Ruby a little squeeze, Ruby felt like a princess.

And whenever Ruby went back to feeling rubbish, because of course she did from time to time . . .

. . . Dot would listen very carefully and help her to sort out her feelings so well, that the warm thing happened in Ruby's tummy again.

And after that, with her new friends, Ruby started visiting the little park at the end of her street. It was full of flowers and ponds.

"Not hanging around the rubbish any more?" asked the dustbin man as he walked by. "No, I prefer being here now," said Ruby, "it's so lovely."

"Just like you,"
said the dustbin man.
"Yes, just like me,"
said Ruby.